Workshop on Automatic Assessment of Atypical Speech (AAAS-2025)

Tallinn, Estonia
5 March 2025

ISBN: 979-8-3313-1884-0

Printed from e-media with permission by:

Curran Associates, Inc.
57 Morehouse Lane
Red Hook, NY 12571

CURRAN ASSOCIATES INC. proceedings.com

Some format issues inherent in the e-media version may also appear in this print version.

Printed with permission by Curran Associates, Inc. (2026)

Association for Computational Linguistics
209 N. Eighth Street
Stroudsburg, Pennsylvania 18360

Phone: 1-570-476-8006
Fax: 1-570-476-0860

acl@aclweb.org

Additional copies of this publication are available from:

Curran Associates, Inc.
57 Morehouse Lane
Red Hook, NY 12571 USA
Phone: 845-758-0400
Fax: 845-758-2633
Email: curran@proceedings.com
Web: www.proceedings.com

The Workshop on Automatic Assessment of Atypical Speech (AAAS-2025)

Proceedings of the Workshop

March 5, 2025
Tallinn, Estonia

Editors: Mikko Kurimo and Tamas Grosz

The AAAS-2025 organizers gratefully acknowledge the support from NordForsk through the funding to "Technology-enhanced foreign and second-language learning of Nordic languages (TEFLON)", project number 103893.

Published by:
University of Tartu Library, Estonia
Indexed in the ACL Anthology

Editors: Mikko Kurimo and Tamas Grosz

Message from the Workshop Chair

The workshop on Automatic Assessment of Atypical Speech (AAAS) explores the assessment of pronunciation and speaking skills of children, language learners, and speakers with speech sound disorders and methods to provide automatic rating and feedback using automatic speech recognition (ASR) and large language models (LLMs). The workshop takes place in Tallinn, Estonia, on March 5th, 2025, in a physical setting, allowing for potential hybrid participation.

Automatic speaking assessment (ASA) is a rapidly growing field that answers to the need for AI tools to self-practise second and foreign language skills. This is not limited to pronunciation assessment, but the AI systems can also provide more complex feedback about fluency, vocabulary and grammar of the recorded speech. ASA is also very relevant for the detection and quantification of speech disorders and for developing speech exercises that can be performed independently at home. The important applications of processing non-standard speech also include interfaces for children and elderly speakers as an alternative to using text input and output. The topic is timely, because the latest large speech models allow us now to develop ASR and classification methods for low-resourced data, such as atypical speech, where annotated training datasets are rarely available, expensive and difficult to transcribe, rate and share.

The idea to organize this workshop came during the last year of a 4-year long research project TEFLON with partners from Finland, Sweden and Norway. The project has been funded by NordForsk's programme for multidisciplinary research collaboration in Nordic countries and it focused on gamified pronunciation training and assessment for children learning Nordic languages. The goal of this workshop is to present the latest results in the field of ASA and discuss the future work and collaboration between the researchers in Nordic and Baltic countries.

In the call for papers, we invited students, researchers, and other experts and stakeholders to contribute papers and/or join the discussion on the following (and related) topics:

- Automatic speaking assessment (ASA) for L2 (second or foreign language) pronunciation
- ASA for spoken L2 proficiency
- ASA for speech sound disorders (SSD)
- Automatic speech recognition (ASR) for L2 learners

- ASR for children and young L2 learners
- ASA and ASR for Nordic and other low-resource languages and tasks
- Spoken L2 learning and speech therapy using games
- Automatic generation of verbal feedback for spoken L2 learners using LLMs

In total 7 submissions were received of which 4 were archival submissions. The programme committee (PC) consisted of 27 members (excluding the 3 program chairs), who served as reviewers providing at least 3 reviews for each archival submission. Based on the PC assessments regarding the content, and quality of the submissions, the program chairs decided to accept only 2 submissions for presentation and publication. The non-archival submissions were presentation abstracts of related projects in Finland and Estonia. These 3 project presentation submissions, 2 peer-reviewed research papers, 1 invited presentation from the TEFLON project and 2 other invited talks together compose our workshop programme consisting of 8 talks and a panel discussion.

To complete the programme we invited 3 keynote talks to strengthen the connection of the speaking assessment research to its main application fields: in speech therapy by Nina Benway (University of Maryland, USA) and second language proficiency assessment Ari Huhta (University of Jyväskylä, Finland). For the third keynote talk we invited all the partners of the TEFLON project to briefly present their key results.

Thank you to everyone for being part of AAAS-2025, and I wish you a wonderful workshop!

Mikko Kurimo, Workshop Chair
Espoo
February 2025

Organizers

Workshop Chair

Mikko Kurimo, Aalto University, Finland

Workshop Organizers

Mikko Kurimo, Aalto University, Finland
Giampiero Salvi, NTNU
Sofia Strömbergsson, Karolinska Institutet
Sari Ylinen, Tampere University
Minna Lehtonen, University of Turku
Tamas Grosz, Aalto University
Ekaterina Voskoboinik, Aalto University
Yaroslav Getman, Aalto University
Nhan Phan, Aalto University

Program Chairs

Mikko Kurimo, Aalto University, Finland
Tamas Grosz, Aalto University, Finland
Simon King, University of Edinburgh, UK

Program Committee

Adriana Stan, Anna Smolander, Catia Cucchiarini, Ekaterina Voskoboinik, Geza Nemeth, Giampiero Salvi, Helmer Strik, Horia Cucu, Hugo Van Hamme, Katalin Mády, Klaus Zechner, Mathew Magimai Doss, Mikko Kurimo (chair), Mikko Kuronen, Minna Lehtonen, Mittul Singh, Nhan Phan, Paavo Alku, Pablo Riera, Ragheb Al-Ghezi, Raili Hilden, Riikka Ullakonoja, Sari Ylinen, Shahin Amiriparian, Simon King (co-chair), Sneha Das, Sofia Strömbergsson, Tamás Grósz (co-chair), Tanel Alumäe, Yaroslav Getman

Invited Talk: What is so hard about AI Speech Therapy? Evidence from Efficacy Trials

Nina R Benway
University of Maryland, College Park

Artificial intelligence (AI) speech therapy systems hold significant potential for individuals seeking to acquire and generalize speech sound motor plans through targeted intervention. Research indicates that approximately 5,000 speech therapy practice trials are required to generalize a newly acquired speech motor plan to continuous speech [1, 2]. However, access to sufficiently intensive intervention remains a challenge worldwide [3-6], with the actual dosage of therapy often falling well below evidence-based recommendations [7-9]. AI speech therapy systems could help bridge this gap by enabling at-home, independent practice and automated feedback that aligns with best-practice intensity levels and therapeutic paradigms [10]. While recent technological advancements have begun to overcome key technical barriers like child speech data scarcity and limited technical transparency, important questions remain regarding the therapeutic efficacy of AI clinicians. High-quality clinical trials are now emerging, offering critical insights into the real-world effectiveness and therapeutic impact of AI-driven speech therapy tools [11, 12].

It is important to critically examine the rigor of these clinical trials and the broader implications they pose for the future of AI speech therapy. Key questions include: What clinical results do developers need to report to show that their systems are fit-for-purpose? How do AI-driven speech analysis and intervention systems compare to human clinician judgment in real-world settings? Which speech errors are most appropriate for automated analysis? What child profiles are best suited for ethical independent speech practice? What preferences and difficulties do users have with regard to AI clinicians? This presentation explores both the promise and limitations of AI-driven speech therapy through the lens of systematic review [13-16], recently completed small-n and randomized efficacy trials [11, 12], and our ongoing randomized controlled trials.

References

[1] Koegel, L.K., R. Koegel, L., and J.C. Ingham, *Programming Rapid Generalization of Correct Articulation through Self-Monitoring Procedures.* Journal of Speech and Hearing Disorders, 1986. 51(1): p. 24-32.

[2] Koegel, R., L., et al., *Within-Clinic versus Outside-of-Clinic Self-Monitoring of Articulation to Promote Generalization.* Journal of Speech and Hearing Disorders, 1988. 53(4): p. 392-399.
[3] Health Workforce Australia, *Speech Pathologists in Focus*, in *Australia's Health Workforce Series*, Department of Health, Editor. 2014.
[4] Verdon, S., et al., *An investigation of equity of rural speech-language pathology services for children: A geographic perspective.* International Journal of Speech-Language Pathology, 2011. 13(3): p. 239-250.
[5] Sugden, E., et al., *Service delivery and intervention intensity for phonology-based speech sound disorders.* Int J Lang Commun Disord, 2018. 53(4): p. 718-734.
[6] Pring, T., et al., *The working practices and clinical experiences of paediatric speech and language therapists: A national UK survey.* International Journal of Language & Communication Disorders, 2012. 47(6): p. 696-708.
[7] Preston, J.L., et al., *A Randomized Controlled Trial of Treatment Distribution and Biofeedback Effects on Speech Production in School-Age Children With Apraxia of Speech.* Journal of Speech, Language, and Hearing Research, 2024. 67(9s).
[8] Kaipa, R. and A.M. Peterson, *A systematic review of treatment intensity in speech disorders.* Int J Speech Lang Pathol, 2016. 18(6): p. 507-520.
[9] Allen, M.M., *Intervention efficacy and intensity for children with speech sound disorder.* J Speech Lang Hear Res, 2013. 56(3): p. 865-77.
[10] Maas, E., et al., *Principles of motor learning in treatment of motor speech disorders.* Am J Speech Lang Pathol, 2008. 17(3): p. 277-98.
[11] Hair, A., et al., *A Longitudinal Evaluation of Tablet-Based Child Speech Therapy with Apraxia World.* ACM Trans. Access. Comput., 2021. 14(1).
[12] Benway, N.R. and J.L. Preston, *Artificial Intelligence Assisted Speech Therapy for /ɹ/ using Speech Motor Chaining and the PERCEPT Engine: a Single Case Experimental Clinical Trial with ChainingAI.* American Journal of Speech-Language Pathology, 2024. 33(5): p. 2461-2486.
[13] Deka, C., et al., *AI-based automated speech therapy tools for persons with speech sound disorder: a systematic literature review.* Speech, Language and Hearing, 2024: p. 1-22.
[14] McKechnie, J., et al., *Automated speech analysis tools for children's speech production: A systematic literature review.* International Journal of Speech Language Pathology, 2018. 20(6): p. 583-598.
[15] Furlong, L., et al., *Mobile apps for treatment of speech disorders in children: An evidence-based analysis of quality and efficacy.* PLOS ONE, 2018. 13(8): p. e0201513.
[16] Chen, Y.-P.P., et al., *Systematic review of virtual speech therapists for speech disorders.* Computer Speech & Language, 2016. 37: p. 98-128.

Invited Talk: Automatic assessment of second/foreign language speaking: Review of developments for examination and teaching/learning purposes

Ari Huhta
University of Jyväskylä

The presentation focuses on describing how automatic assessment of second/foreign language (L2) speech has advanced due to innovations in speech processing, machine learning, and natural language processing (NLP). Modern systems evaluate pronunciation, fluency, prosody, and intelligibility using a combination of acoustic, linguistic, and prosodic features (e.g.[3, 5]).

Advances in artificial intelligence (AI) have led to improvements in assessment accuracy. These advancements have been integrated into commercial applications, including TOEFL®, Pearson's Versant, Duolingo English Test, and AI-driven tutoring systems like ELSA Speak. While English is still the most common language assessed automatically, significant developments are taking place also for many other languages (e.g. [1, 2, 4]).

Despite progress, challenges remain in data scarcity, accent robustness, bias mitigation, and adaptive feedback. Current systems still struggle with diverse L2 accents and ensuring fairness in automated scoring. Future developments are likely to focus on multimodal integration (speech, facial expressions, gestures), explainable AI feedback, and personalized adaptive learning models to improve language learning experiences.

References

[1] Al-Ghezi, R., Voskoboinik, K., Getman, Y., von Zansen, A., Kallio, H., Kurimo, M., Huhta, A., & Hildén, R. (2023). Automatic Speaking Assessment of Spontaneous L2 Finnish and Swedish. *Language Assessment Quarterly, 20*(4-5), 421-444.
[2] Farrús, M. 2023. Automatic Speech Recognition in L2 learning: A review based on PRISMA methodology. Languages 8:242. https://doi.org/10.3390/languages8040242
[3] Wu, X-Y. 2024. Artificial Intelligence in L2 learning: A meta-analysis of contextual, instructional, and social-emotional moderators. System 126, 103498.
[4] Wu, Y. & Shen, X. 2024. The assessment of automated rating of L2 Mandarin prosody in lexical tone recognition and pauses. Speech Prosody, Leiden, The Netherlands. 250-254. https://www.isca-archive.org/speechprosody_2024/wu24_speechprosody.pdf
[5] Zecher, K. & Evanini, K. (Eds.) 2020. Automated speaking assessment. Using language technologies to score spontaneous speech. Routledge.

Table of Contents

Investigating Further Fine-tuning Wav2vec2.0 in Low Resource Settings for Enhancing Children Speech Recognition and Word-level Reading Diagnosis

Lingyun Gao, Cristian Tejedor-Garcia, Catia Cucchiarini, Helmer Strik
Centre for Language Studies
Radboud University, Nijmegen, the Netherlands
{lingyun.gao, cristian.tejedorgarcia, catia.cucchiarini, helmer.strik}@ru.nl

Abstract

Automatic reading diagnosis systems can substantially improves teachers' efficiency in scoring reading exercises and provide students with easier access to reading practice and feedback. However, few studies have focused on developing Automatic Speech Recognition (ASR)-based reading diagnosis systems due mainly to scarcity of data. This study explores the effectiveness and robustness of further fine-tuning the Wav2vec2.0 large model in low-resource settings, for recognizing children speech and detecting reading miscues using target domain and similar out-of-domain data. Our results show a word error rate (WER) of 10.9% and an F1 score of 0.49 for reading miscue detection achieved by our best fine-tuned model training with target domain data, while using similar out-of-domain non-native read speech can enhance the model performance for unseen speakers and noisy settings. The analyses provide insights into the robustness of further fine-tuning strategies on the Wav2vec2.0 model.

1 Introduction

Recent advances in Automatic Speech Recognition (ASR) have made many previously complex speech–based computer-assisted applications more feasible (Ivanko et al., 2023). One such application is the integration of ASR into primary school reading education (Shadiev and Liu, 2023). However, this initiative has encountered significant challenges in children speech recognition (Feng et al., 2024) and miscue detection (Shivakumar and Narayanan, 2022), largely due to the scarcity of speech data and annotations, especially for languages other than English.

Meanwhile, growing concerns over declining reading proficiency levels among low-resource language users (Swart et al., 2023) highlight the urgent need for innovative approaches to improve reading instruction. A common task in reading education is miscue detection (Limonard et al., 2020), which involves two steps: first, identifying general reading errors such as word substitution, insertion, and deletion, and second, classifying specific miscues, including various types of substitution and insertion errors (Shivakumar and Narayanan, 2022). This process requires the manual transcription of mispronunciations and the annotation of miscue categories, making data collection both time-consuming and costly.

State-of-the-art (SOTA) large pretrained ASR models have shown remarkable performance in adult speech recognition (Pratap et al., 2024) and offer potential for supporting practice and remedial teaching (Molenaar et al., 2023) in low-resource children's reading education. Wav2Vec 2.0-CTC and similar models are especially promising due to their ability to detect spoken errors more accurately (Gao et al., 2024). Research has also shown Wav2Vec 2.0's effectiveness in low-resource transfer learning tasks, improving children's speech recognition in English through fine-tuning pretrained models (Bartelds et al., 2023; Jain et al., 2023). For Dutch child speech, data augmentation with cross-lingual speaker diversity has proven effective, though it mainly benefits unseen speaker recognition (Zhang et al., 2024). However, these methods require significant computational resources and training data. Given the high cost of child speech data collection and ASR model training, further fine-tuning (Shen et al., 2021) trained ASR models offers a low-cost alternative by leveraging knowledge from adult speech, making it particularly suitable for low-resource languages. Moreover, previous research has shown that speech data from similar domains

Proceedings of AAAS Workshop 2025 – Automatic Assessment of Atypical Speech, pages 1–6
March 5, 2025

can be effectively used as augmentation for target domain speech recognition. In (San et al., 2024), training ASR with speech data from similar languages or accents has been found to improve target language speech recognition in low-resource settings. Nevertheless, further finetuning and augmentation with similar domain data has not been extensively explored in the context of Dutch children speech recognition and the impact of this method on downstream reading diagnosis.

In addition, most existing fine-tuning and augmentation studies have employed clean datasets, often collected in laboratories, while real-world child reading exercises typically take place in home and classrooms with diverse background noise and other environmental factors (Lavechin et al., 2020). The robustness of these strategies on ASR for real-world Dutch children's read speech remains unclear.

In this work, we make a novel contribution by filling the gap of investigating the effectiveness of further fine-tuning Dutch adult speech trained Wav2vec2.0, using target domain and similar out-of-domain data, for Dutch native child read speech recognition and reading miscue detection. Additionally, we address the research gap of exploring robustness of further fine-tuning in diverse real-world reading tasks and context where Dutch primary pupils read aloud. The research questions we address in our study are:

RQ1: *To what extent can low-resource further fine-tuning of the adult-speech trained Wav2vec2.0 model enhance the performance of Dutch native children's read speech recognition?*

RQ2: *To what extent can similar out-of-domain (native child dialogue and non-native child read speech) data used in further fine-tuning improve target-domain Dutch native children's read speech recognition?*

RQ3: *To what extent can the above mentioned further fine-tuning strategies enhance Dutch children's reading miscue detection?*

RQ4: *To what extent are the above-mentioned further fine-tuning strategies robust to real-world Dutch native children's read speech recognition?*

We address our research questions through a two-phase study. In the first phase, we explore the efficacy of different fine-tuning options on clean child read speech recognition. In the second phase, we select models representing effective training strategies for experiments on investigating the robustness of real-world child read speech and their ability to detect children's reading miscue.

Table 1: Reading error categories and reading miscue categories with their abbreviations in brackets

Error Type	Reading Miscue Type	Other
Substitution	Substitute a word in the prompt by another existing dutch word which was semantically identical (**SS**)	-
	Substitute a word in prompt by another existing dutch word which was orthographically similar (**OS**)	-
	Replace a word in prompt by another existing dutch word which was not orthographically or semantically similar (**O**)	-
Insertion		Restart
	Insertion of an extra word not in the prompt ($\boldsymbol{I_m}$)	-
Deletion	a word in the prompt is not read (**D**)	-

2 Methodology

2.1 Dataset and Preprocessing

This paper utilizes clean children speech from the Jasmin-CGN Corpus (Cucchiarini et al., 2008), and real-world Dutch child read speech from DART (Bai et al., 2021) and ST.CART (Wills et al., 2023). In the Jasmin-CGN Corpus, the target domain data, the native children read speech subset, includes recordings of 71 primary school children (ages 6-13, reading level 1-9) reading aloud at their mastery reading level, aligned with manual orthographic transcriptions. Children of the same reading level share the same reading prompt. Each prompt consists of three stories. The recordings of the first prompt story are aligned with the prompt text, reading miscue, and reading strategy annotations (data description available in (Limonard et al., 2020)). The native child dialogue speech and non-native child reading speech are used as similar out-of-domain data for augmentation. The native child dialogue speech consists of recordings of the same 71 speakers. The non-native child read speech consists of read speech from 53 non-native primary school children.

To investigate the impact of fine-tuning with different data on recognizing child speech, we split the Jasmin dataset, as shown in Table 2, into validation, training, and testing subsets. We created two child speech test sets: the full test set and the non-overlap test set. The full test set includes speakers overlapping with those in the training data, while the non-overlap test set consists of independent speakers. These test sets allow us to assess the ability of fine-tuning to handle unseen

Table 2: Data split details for Jasmin-CGN Corpus

Dataset Split	Content	Duration
Validation Set	Read Speech (story 2&3): First five samples from each of 65 native speakers.	31 minutes
Train:clean-FULL	Read Speech (story 2&3): Remaining sentences from 65 native speakers after validation samples are excluded.	4.4 hours
Train:clean-aug-nonna	Augmented set including native and non-native read speech.	8 hours
Train:clean-aug-dial	Augmented set including native read and child-only dialogue speech.	8 hours
Train:clean-SDS	Read Speech (story 2&3): Samples from the sentence order 8th to 20th	~1 hour
Train:clean-SPDS	Read Speech (story 2&3): Random selection of sentence samples from 65 speakers emphasizing mispronunciations.	~1 hour
Test:clean (Full)	Read Speech (story no.1): First prompt readings from all 65 speakers (71 recordings).	2.05 hours
Test:clean (Non-overlap)	Read Speech (story no.1): First prompt readings from six other speakers, avoiding overlap with the 65 speakers.	14 minutes

speakers.

Real-world speech recordings are more complex than speech recorded in a controlled lab setting, as it includes diverse speaking conditions and environmental noise. In this paper, we use the following two datasets to represent real-world speech. The DART test dataset consists of children reading speech recorded at home, primarily featuring environmental noise from different microphones and parents' voices. The ST.CART test dataset consists of children's reading speech recorded in a classroom, mainly including background noise from other children talking and reading. In both real-world datasets, usually the volume of speech is less well-controlled, and children are less attentive, leading to greater variation in speech speed compared to recordings made in a lab.

For evaluating fine-tuning robustness, we used three real-world testsets from DART and ST.CART. The DART test dataset, with 48 minutes of Dutch children reading sentences and stories at home, assesses robustness on real-world data seen during validation, but not included in training. The validation set includes 3 minutes of sentence recordings and 2.5 minutes of story recordings, while the DART testset includes 15 minutes of sentence recordings and 33 minutes of story recordings. The ST.CART testset, consisting of 36 minutes of Dutch children reading stories in classrooms, evaluates robustness on real-world data that was not seen during any training phase.

2.2 Reading Miscue Detection

In this paper, word-level reading errors include substitutions, insertions, and deletions. Word-level reading miscues, which are a subset of these errors, encompass specific substitution and insertion errors, as detailed in (Limonard et al., 2020) and shown in Table 1. Insertions in reading miscues are a subset of insertion errors, but correct readings after restarts or repetitions are not classified as insertion miscues, in line with Dutch reading test conventions (van Til et al., 2018).

For evaluating fine-tuned models, we focus on detecting word-level reading miscues, defined as errors where both the type and location match between prediction and ground truth. Analysis is based on detected general errors from manual transcriptions and ASR outputs, with miscue categorization outlined in Table 1. We follow the steps in section 2.3 of (Gao et al., 2024) to obtain and evaluate miscue labels.

2.3 ASR Models, Metrics and Tools

We evaluate the effectiveness of further finetuning ASR models in recognizing Dutch native children speech and detecting word-level reading miscues. The ASR foundation model Wav2vec2.0 we used in this paper is pretrained and finetuned with Dutch adult speech. We would like to further finetune the ASR model with Dutch child. ASR models are employed to predict word-level transcriptions, coupled with the Speech Recognition Toolkit SCTK (Lütkebohle, 2021). We employ Word Error Rate (WER) for evaluating children speech recognition at each testset and Precision, Recall, F1 for reading miscue detection evaluation, similarly in our previous work(Gao et al., 2024).

We (further) fine-tune the Wav2vec2.0 large model on different training dataset sourced from the Jasmin-CGN Dutch children speech. Our (further) fine-tuning experiments use hyperparameters similar to those reported by (Baevski et al., 2020) for comparable data sizes. In order to train models on a single A6000 GPU, following training settings in (Bartelds et al., 2023), We train the models with a batch size of 4 or 8 and apply gradient accumulation steps of 8 or 4, respectively, over 10k steps, using a learning rate of 1e-5 and a single seed.

3 Results

3.1 Performance on Different Fine-Tuning Options

We address RQ1 and RQ2 by evaluating further fine-tuning strategies on Wav2vec2.0 for children speech recognition performance, measured by WER, using different training datasets. The results are shown in Table 3. The baseline model is the Dutch adult pretrained Wav2vec2.0 fine-tuned on adult read speech, without further finetuning on child data.

Table 3: Evaluation of children speech recognition by WER of the baseline and fine-tuned models with different training sets.

Model	test-clean	
	full	non-overlap
RQ1		
pretrain-adult-ft-adult	13.2	13.9
pretrain-adult-ft-adult-clean-FULL	**10.9**	12.2
pretrain-adult-ft-adult-clean-SPDS	11.1	11.7
pretrain-adult-ft-adult-clean-SDS	11.3	11.7
RQ2		
pretrain-adult-ft-adult-clean-aug-dial	11.4	12.1
pretrain-adult-ft-adult-clean-aug-nonna	11.5	**11.2**

For RQ1, our results highlight that fine-tuning with a small dataset of Dutch native children's read speech (clean-FULL: 4.4 hours) can substantially enhance the model's accuracy for this demographic (WER=10.9%, absolute improvement=2.3%, Table 3). Meanwhile, using a speaker-prompt train subset SPDS can achieve competitive performance overall (WER=11.1% vs 10.9%) and improve results for unseen speakers (WER=11.7% vs 12.2%), underscoring the importance of data diversity in fine-tuning rather than sheer volume.

For RQ2, our findings show that further fine-tuning with non-native read speech augmentation improves recognition for unseen child speakers (best WER=11.2%, compared to 12.2% with clean-FULL fine-tuning on test-clean non-overlap), emphasizing the benefit of increased speaker diversity through out-of-domain data. However, on the test-clean full set, where speakers largely overlapped with the training data, neither fine-tuning with native dialogue augmentation (WER=11.4%) nor non-native speech data (WER=11.5%) improved performance over the clean-FULL model (WER=10.9%), as shown in the bottom part of Table 3, suggesting a significant domain transfer gap between dialogue and read speech for training ASR models, consistent with (Proença et al., 2018).

3.2 Detection of Reading Miscues

Then, to address RQ3, we compare precision, recall, and F1 scores of different models for miscue detection in Table 4. Our results confirm the effectiveness of low-resource fine-tuning with target-domain read speech and one out-of-domain (non-native) data in improving Dutch children's miscue detection. The best detection performance on the full testset was achieved by further fine-tuning with clean-full (F1=0.49), while the non-overlap testset was best handled by fine-tuning with clean-aug-nonna (F1=0.57), compared to 0.43 and 0.44 respectively for the baseline model. This trend mirrors WER improvements, indicating a strong correlation between speech recognition performance and miscue detection.

3.3 Robustness to Real-World Data and Reading Tasks

To address RQ4, we compare the WER performance of models trained with different strategies against a baseline model without further fine-tuning across three real-world testsets, as shown in Table 5. Our findings indicate that further fine-tuning strategies show limited robustness to unseen real-world data, as all fine-tuned models performed worse in these cases. In particular, the fine-tuning strategies, ft-adult-clean-FULL and ft-adult-clean-aug-dial, substantially improve WER on datasets similar to the training data (50.4% and 50.7%, respectively). On the unseen DART story testset, ft-adult-clean-aug-dial achieves the best performance with a WER of 39.0%. However, these models face challenges in generalizing to the ST.CART story test set. All fine-tuned models, including ft-adult-clean-FULL and ft-adult-clean-aug-nonna, underperform compared to the baseline (WER = 39.5%). This highlights a trade-off between in-domain optimization and broader generalization, as fine-tuning on small, clean datasets tends to reduce the model's ability to generalize effectively. Despite this, the results suggest that incorporating a limited amount of real-world data into the validation set can enhance the effectiveness of fine-tuning. Specifically, the strategy involving dialogue augmentation demonstrated the highest robustness among the various fine-tuning approaches.

Table 4: ASR model performance in reading miscue detection, evaluated by precision (P), recall (R), and F1 on the full testset and speaker-independent subset, with F1 for each miscue category in Table 1.

Model	All miscues				I_m	D	OS	SS	O
	P(full)	R(full)	F1(full)	F1(non-overlap)	F1	F1	F1	F1	F1
pretrain-adult-ft-adult	0.29	0.83	0.43	0.44	0.63	**0.59**	0.17	0.39	0.28
pretrain-adult-ft-adult-clean-FULL	**0.35**	**0.83**	**0.49**	0.54	0.71	**0.59**	**0.22**	0.4	**0.35**
pretrain-adult-ft-adult-clean-SPDS	0.34	0.83	0.48	0.55	**0.74**	0.57	0.20	**0.42**	0.33
pretrain-adult-ft-adult-clean-aug-dial	0.33	0.82	0.47	0.51	0.67	0.56	0.21	0.4	0.33
pretrain-adult-ft-adult-clean-aug-nonna	0.33	0.83	0.47	**0.57**	0.73	0.54	0.21	0.36	0.32

Table 5: ASR model evaluated by WER in three real-world test dataset

Model	DART		ST.CART
	sentence	story	story
ft-adult	62.4	53.2	**39.5**
ft-adult-clean-FULL	**50.4**	39.8	48.6
ft-adult-clean-SPDS	53.8	43.0	43.7
ft-adult-clean-aug-dial	50.7	**39.0**	44.5
ft-adult-clean-aug-nonna	55.2	40.1	51.4

4 Conclusion

This study demonstrates the potential of further fine-tuning the Wav2vec2.0 large model with domain-specific data to improve read speech recognition in Dutch native children. It highlights the effectiveness of augmenting training data with similar out-of-domain data, especially for unseen speakers in clean settings and real-world scenarios if a small amount of real-world audio can be utilized for validation.

Acknowledgments

This work was supported by the NWO research programme AiNed Fellowship Grants under the project Responsible AI for Voice Diagnostics (RAIVD) - NGF.1607.22.013.

References

Alexei Baevski, Yuhao Zhou, Abdelrahman Mohamed, and Michael Auli. 2020. wav2vec 2.0: A framework for self-supervised learning of speech representations. *Advances in neural information processing systems*, 33:12449–12460.

Yu Bai, Ferdy Hubers, Catia Cucchiarini, and Helmer Strik. 2021. An asr-based reading tutor for practicing reading skills in the first grade: Improving performance through threshold adjustment. In *IberSPEECH 2021*, pages 11–15.

Martijn Bartelds, Nay San, Bradley McDonnell, Dan Jurafsky, and Martijn Wieling. 2023. Making more of little data: Improving low-resource automatic speech recognition using data augmentation. In *Proceedings of the 61st Annual Meeting of the ACL*, pages 715–729, Toronto, Canada. Association for Computational Linguistics.

Catia Cucchiarini, Joris Driesen, Hugo Van hamme, and Eric Sanders. 2008. Recording speech of children, non-natives and elderly people for HLT applications: the JASMIN-CGN corpus. In *Proceedings of the Sixth International Conference on Language Resources and Evaluation (LREC'08)*, Marrakech, Morocco. European Language Resources Association (ELRA).

Siyuan Feng, Bence Mark Halpern, Olya Kudina, and Odette Scharenborg. 2024. Towards inclusive automatic speech recognition. *Computer Speech & Language*, 84:101567.

Lingyun Gao, Cristian Tejedor-Garcia, Helmer Strik, and Catia Cucchiarini. 2024. Reading miscue detection in primary school through automatic speech recognition. In *Interspeech 2024*, pages 5153–5157.

Denis Ivanko, Dmitry Ryumin, and Alexey Karpov. 2023. A review of recent advances on deep learning methods for audio-visual speech recognition. *Mathematics*, 11(12):2665.

Rishabh Jain, Andrei Barcovschi, Mariam Yahayah Yiwere, Dan Bigioi, Peter Corcoran, and Horia Cucu. 2023. A wav2vec2-based experimental study on self-supervised learning methods to improve child speech recognition. *IEEE Access*, 11:46938–46948.

Marvin Lavechin, Ruben Bousbib, Hervé Bredin, Emmanuel Dupoux, and Alejandrina Cristia. 2020. An open-source voice type classifier for child-centered daylong recordings. In *Interspeech*.

S. Limonard, Catia Cucchiarini, R.W.N.M. van Hout, and Helmer Strik. 2020. Analyzing read aloud speech by primary school pupils: Insights for research and development. In *Interspeech 2020*, pages 3710–3714.

Ingo Lütkebohle. 2021. The nist speech recognition scoring toolkit (sctk) 2.4.12. https://github.com/usnistgov/SCTK. [Online; accessed 10-March-2024].

Bo Molenaar, Cristian Tejedor-Garcia, Catia Cucchiarini, and Helmer Strik. 2023. Automatic Assessment of Oral Reading Accuracy for Reading Diagnostics. In *Proc. INTERSPEECH 2023*, pages 5232–5236.

Vineel Pratap, Andros Tjandra, Bowen Shi, Paden Tomasello, Arun Babu, Sayani Kundu, Ali Elkahky, Zhaoheng Ni, Apoorv Vyas, Maryam Fazel-Zarandi, et al. 2024. Scaling speech technology to 1,000+ languages. *Journal of Machine Learning Research*, 25(97):1–52.

Jorge Proença, Carla Lopes, Michael Tjalve, Andreas Stolcke, Sara Candeias, and Fernando Perdigao. 2018. Mispronunciation detection in children's reading of sentences. *IEEE/ACM Transactions on Audio, Speech, and Language Processing*, 26(7):1207–1219.

Nay San, Georgios Paraskevopoulos, Aryaman Arora, Xiluo He, Prabhjot Kaur, Oliver Adams, and Dan Jurafsky. 2024. Predicting positive transfer for improved low-resource speech recognition using acoustic pseudo-tokens. In *Proceedings of the 6th Workshop on Research in Computational Linguistic Typology and Multilingual NLP*, pages 100–112, St. Julian's, Malta. Association for Computational Linguistics.

Rustam Shadiev and Jiawen Liu. 2023. Review of research on applications of speech recognition technology to assist language learning. *ReCALL*, 35(1):74–88.

Zhiqiang Shen, Zechun Liu, Jie Qin, Marios Savvides, and Kwang-Ting Cheng. 2021. Partial is better than all: Revisiting fine-tuning strategy for few-shot learning. In *Proceedings of the AAAI conference on artificial intelligence*, volume 35, pages 9594–9602.

Prashanth Gurunath Shivakumar and Shrikanth Narayanan. 2022. End-to-end neural systems for automatic children speech recognition: An empirical study. *Computer Speech & Language*, 72:101289.

Nicole Swart, Joyce. Gubbels, Melissa in 't Zandt, Maarten Wolbers, and Eliane Segers. 2023. PIRLS-2021: Trends in leesprestaties, leesattitude en leesgedrag van tienjarigen uit Nederland.

Alma van Til, Frans Kamphuis, Jos Keuning, Martine Gijsel, Judith Vloedgraven, and Anja de Wijs. 2018. Wetenschappelijke verantwoording lvs-toetsen dmt. *Arnhem: Cito*.

Simone Wills, Cristian Tejedor-Garcia, Catia Cucchiarini, and Helmer Strik. 2023. Enhancing asr-based educational applications: Peer evaluation of non-native child speech. In *9th Workshop on Speech and Language Technology in Education (SLaTE)*, pages 16–20.

Yuanyuan Zhang, Zhengjun Yue, Tanvina Patel, and Odette Scharenborg. 2024. Improving child speech recognition with augmented child-like speech. In *Interspeech 2024*, pages 5183–5187.

Leveraging Uncertainty for Finnish L2 Speech Scoring with LLMs

Ekaterina Voskoboinik, Nhan Phan, Tamás Grósz, Mikko Kurimo
Department of Information and Communications Engineering
Aalto University, Finland
firstname.lastname@aalto.fi

Abstract

Automatic speech assessment (ASA) supports learning but often requires extensive data, which is scarce for languages with fewer learners. Recent research shows that Large Language Models (LLMs) can generalize to new tasks with minimal training data using in-context learning (ICL). We find LLMs effective in estimating the proficiency of individuals learning Finnish as a second language (L2) when given a few examples of human expert grading. The proficiency grades produced by the model, when evaluating verbatim transcripts from an automatic speech recognition (ASR) system, agree with human ratings at a level comparable to the agreement between the human raters. Our experiments reveal that adding more grading demonstrations in ICL improves the model's accuracy but, counterintuitively, increases its uncertainty when selecting an appropriate proficiency level. We show that this uncertainty can be leveraged further by creating soft labels: instead of assigning the most probable level (hard label), we aggregate the model's confidence across all possible levels, resulting in noticeable performance improvements. Further analysis reveals that the sources of model uncertainty differ across ICL settings. In zero-shot, uncertainty stems from intrinsic response properties, such as proficiency level. In few-shot, it is driven by the relationship between the sample and the demonstrations.

1 Introduction

In this study, we focus on automatically assessing the proficiency of second-language (L2) speakers producing spontaneous Finnish speech. Automatic Speech Assessment (ASA) holds significant potential for supporting language learning. However, ASA systems typically depend on machine learning algorithms, which are challenging to train when the available data is limited or when certain classes (proficiency levels in ASA case) are underrepresented. Consequently, the development of ASA systems may be hindered by the scarcity and class imbalance of annotated data. These challenges are particularly pressing for languages with smaller learner bases, such as Finnish, where data availability is inherently limited. Ironically, these resource-limited languages are likely to benefit the most from automated systems that support language learners.

Early ASA approaches for L2 data used models with hand-crafted features targeting specific aspects of spoken proficiency, such as delivery (pronunciation, fluency), language use (vocabulary, grammar), and content (Zechner et al., 2009; Bernstein et al., 2010; Chen and Zechner, 2011; Xie et al., 2012). These features were selected to align with scoring rubrics, ensuring they were meaningful and interpretable within constructs of communicative competence. Later, these hand-crafted features were replaced by representations extracted by neural networks, leading to improved model performance (Chen et al., 2018; Qian et al., 2019; Yoon and Lee, 2019).

However, both hand-crafted features and traditional neural approaches rely on large amounts of labeled data, which is often scarce for L2 ASA. Pre-trained text and audio models have shown themselves as a successful solution to this issue (Wang et al., 2021; Bannò and Matassoni, 2023). Transformer-based models (Vaswani et al., 2017), like BERT (Devlin, 2018) and wav2vec 2.0 (Baevski et al., 2020), are trained in a self-supervised manner on large unlabeled data to learn meaningful language representations. These mod-

Proceedings of AAAS Workshop 2025 – Automatic Assessment of Atypical Speech, pages 7–15
March 5, 2025

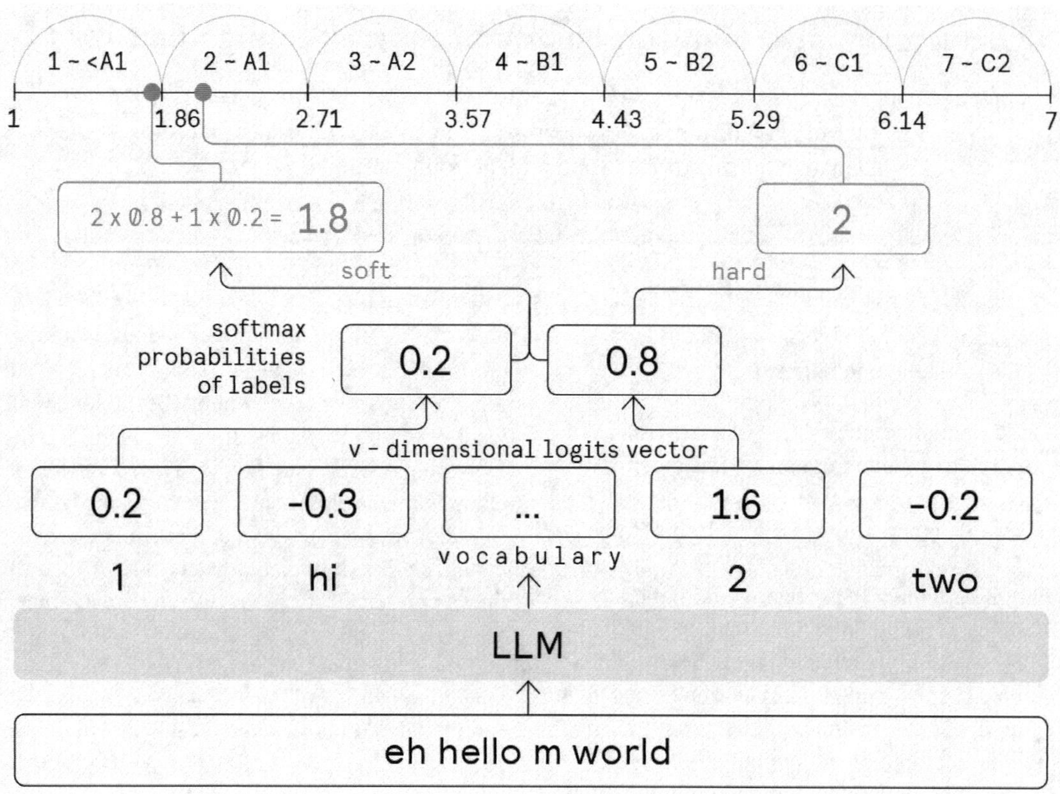

Figure 1: An illustration of assigning a speech sample into two classes through soft and hard labeling. An LLM produces a vector of logits for each token in the vocabulary. The logits corresponding to the class labels (1 and 2) are selected and transformed into a probability distribution using a softmax function. In hard labeling, the class with the highest probability (class 2 with 0.8) is selected. In soft labeling, the probabilities are used as weights: 1 is multiplied by 0.2, and 2 is multiplied by 0.8, resulting in an aggregated score of 1.8. To determine the final level, the aggregated score is mapped to its corresponding bin (bin one in this case as opposed to bin two in hard labeling).

els can then be fine-tuned on smaller datasets for specific tasks. Audio-based models have gained popularity in ASA for bypassing automatic speech recognition (ASR) by directly capturing content, language use, and delivery. They are effective not only for L2 English but also for languages with smaller learner populations, such as Finnish and Finland Swedish (Al-Ghezi et al., 2023). However, these models still face challenges with class imbalance, even when techniques like oversampling and curriculum learning are applied (Lun et al., 2024).

Recent research shows that large language models (LLMs) generalize effectively to tasks with minimal or no annotated data (Radford et al., 2019; Brown, 2020) and possess an implicit understanding of language proficiency (Malik et al., 2024; Kobayashi et al., 2024), making them a promising avenue for addressing the challenges of low-resource Finnish L2 ASA. In this study, we test whether LLMs can effectively differentiate proficiency levels in Finnish L2 speech. We examine how the model's decisions evolve across different in-context learning (ICL) settings (Brown, 2020): where the model is either prompted with the instruction of how to evaluate spoken proficiency or with instructions and grading examples. We observe that while performance improves with more examples, the model becomes less confident in its predictions, distributing probabilities more evenly across levels. To take advantage of this uncertainty, we explore soft labeling, where probabilities across all levels are aggregated as opposed to hard labeling, which assigns only the most probable level. Finally, we analyze the characteristics of responses where soft and hard labels differ, to better understand what makes the model more uncertain and how this uncertainty contributes to grading performance.

2 Data

The data used in this study is a subset of the DigiTala dataset[1], featuring speech samples from learners of Finnish. These samples include responses to semi-structured and open-ended tasks completed by university and upper secondary school students in Finland. Each response was rated on multiple dimensions: pronunciation, fluency, accuracy, range, task completion, and holistically. In this study, we focus on holistic scores as they demonstrated the highest agreement between human raters. The scores range from 1 to 7, corresponding to levels from below A1 to C2 of the Common European Framework of Reference for Languages (CEFR) (Council of Europe, 2001). The CEFR framework evaluates spoken proficiency holistically, encompassing not only delivery features but also language use and content. For samples with multiple ratings, the scores were averaged and mapped to one of seven equal bins within the 1–7 scale to produce an integer score.

For this research, a subset of three tasks was selected based on several criteria: relatively strong human-to-human agreement compared to other tasks (as measured by quadratically weighted kappa (QWK)); task prompts designed to elicit responses of varying lengths; and representation from different student populations (school vs. university). Tasks A and B, performed by school students, involved describing their important place and a library picture, respectively, while Task C, for university students, asked them to talk about their day. When combined, the overall inter-rater agreement across these three tasks, as measured by QWK, is 0.73. Transcriptions were created by human transcribers who recorded speech verbatim, including mispronunciations and hesitations. These transcripts were used to train a wav2vec 2.0 ASR model, which was fine-tuned on native Finnish and then adapted to L2 speech, achieving word and character error rates (WER and CER) of 21.08% and 6.08%, respectively, on the entire L2 Finnish subset of the DigiTala dataset. No external language models or vocabulary were used, allowing the transcripts serve as proxies for certain delivery features, such as mispronunciations.

[1]https://www.kielipankki.fi/corpora/digitala/

	A	B	C
Number of responses	173	63	106
Average duration (s)	43.32	36.00	57.27
QWK	0.50	0.61	0.41
Average score	5.16	4.17	2.80
WER (%)	18	22	35

Table 1: Task Statistics

Table 1 summarizes the statistics for each task. Notably, the QWK values indicate low agreement among human raters, as this metric accounts for the magnitude of disagreements by penalizing larger differences more heavily. Figure 2 shows the imbalanced level distributions, further highlighting the challenge of proficiency scoring for data-driven algorithms.

3 Methods

3.1 Prompting and In-context Learning

LLMs solve tasks through next-token prediction, guided by an input text or "prompt" that specifies the task or instructions. In zero-shot prompting, the model receives only instructions on how to perform a task, without examples. In contrast, in-context learning (ICL) includes demonstrations: one-shot provides a single example, and few-shot offers multiple. For ASA proficiency scoring with LLMs used in this work, an example consists of a response ASR transcript and its corresponding score from human raters.

Chat-tuned models (Touvron et al., 2023) utilize prompts designed to simulate conversational roles, marked by special tokens for system, user, and assistant turns. In this format, the system message contains grading instructions, the user message provides the response transcript, and the assistant message delivers the score. In zero-shot prompts, only system and user messages are included, whereas in ICL, user-assistant message pairs with human grading examples are also injected. The example of one-shot prompt with a chat-tuned model is given in Figure 3.

3.2 Hard vs Soft Labeling

Instead of relying on the model to generate an output score directly or selecting the most probable level token (hard labeling), we use a soft labeling approach by aggregating the model's confidence

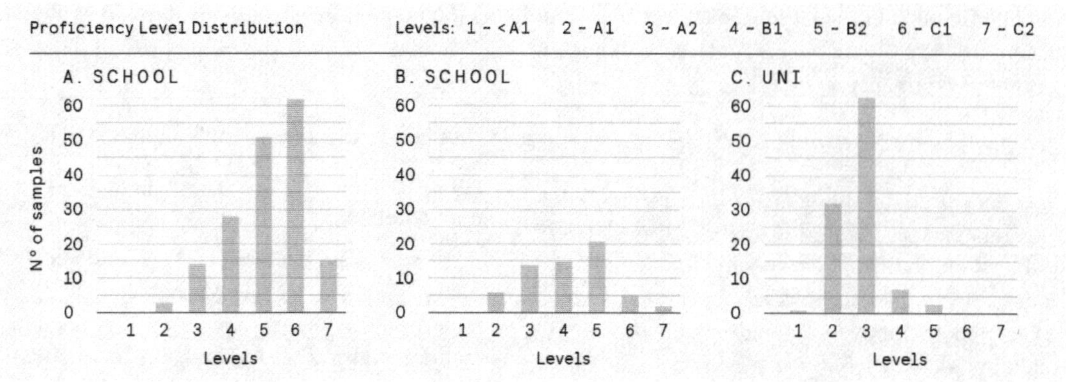

Figure 2: The distribution of responses with different proficiency levels among the tasks.

across all possible proficiency levels. We first collect logits for each level, then apply the softmax function to convert them into a probability distribution. This distribution is used to compute a weighted average label. For example, if the model assigns 80% confidence to level 2 and 20% to level 1, the weighted average is 1.8. This score is then mapped to the bins used for converting average human ratings to integers. Figure 1 illustrates the soft labeling process.

3.3 Entropy as Model's Uncertainty Measure

Entropy measures the uncertainty in a probability distribution. When probability mass is concentrated on one class, entropy is low; when all labels are equally likely, entropy is high. We compute entropy for the proficiency label space (1-7) using logits from the model's next-token prediction:

$$\text{Entropy} = -\sum_{i=1}^{n} P(x_i) \log P(x_i)$$

where n is the number of labels (7), and $P(x_i)$ is the probability of label i after applying softmax. This reflects the uncertainty of the model when determining which proficiency level to assign to a student response.

3.4 Response Characteristics

Here, we describe the response properties explored in relation to their influence on model uncertainty.

Perplexity: Perplexity (ppl) measures how "surprised" a language model is by a sequence of tokens, with lower values indicating that the model can predict the next token more accurately. We calculate it as the exponentiated average negative log-likelihood of the tokens in the user message, conditioned on the previous prompt:

$$\text{Perplexity} = \exp\left(-\frac{1}{t}\sum_{i=1}^{t} \log P(x_i \mid \text{context})\right)$$

where t is the number of tokens in the test sample, x_i are the tokens, and $P(x_i \mid \text{context})$ is the conditional probability given the prompt. The context differs by prompt setting: zero-shot uses only system instructions, while ICL also includes demonstration examples before the sample transcript.

Human Variance: Most recordings received multiple ratings, with raters often disagreeing, as shown by the QWK values in Table 1. We measure this uncertainty using the variance of human scores for each response.

Demonstration Proximity: Prior research suggests that good demonstrations are often semantically close to the graded sample (Liu et al., 2021). We measure this proximity using cosine distance between embeddings generated by the LLM. In the few-shot setting, we calculate the average distance to all the demonstrations. Demonstrations are embedded with human transcripts, while test samples use ASR transcripts. Specifically, we compute embeddings for each token in the transcript using the LLM's encoder and then average these token-level embeddings to create a fixed-length representation for the entire transcript.

CEFR Level: We also use the average unbinned CEFR score to examine whether the model's uncertainty in grading is influenced by the proficiency level of the response.

```
<|begin_of_text|><|start_header_id|>system<|end_header_id|>

You are a system designed to evaluate the language proficiency level of verbal
responses from students learning {language}. Your input will be a verbatim
transcript of their spoken response. Your task is to assign a proficiency level
(ranging from 1 to 7) based on the provided proficiency scale:

{proficiency_scale}

You are required to evaluate responses to the following language test task
instruction:

"{task_description}"

Your response should contain only the level, formatted as follows:
Level: X

Please adhere strictly to this format.<|eot_id|><|start_header_id|>user<|end_
header_id|>

{response_transcript_demonstration}<|eot_id|><|start_header_id|>assistant<|end_
header_id|>

Level: {response_score_demonstration}<|eot_id|><|start_header_id|>user<|end_
header_id|>

{response_transcript}<|eot_id|><|start_header_id|>assistant<|end_header_id|>

Level:
```

Figure 3: Example of a one-shot prompt in a chat-tuned LLM. Text in orange shows the tokens used by the model to differentiate between system, user, and assistant roles.

4 Experiments

4.1 Model and Prompts

Model: The LLM used in this work is Llama 3.1, an 8-billion parameter model tuned for chat.[2]
Prompts: All prompts start with a system message containing instructions to grade proficiency, the grading criteria used by raters, and the task instructions given to students. For the picture task, the picture description was included since the model is text-only. For ICL demonstrations, we selected a response from each score bin with full rater agreement or, if none were available, with minimal disagreement ($\leq$ 1-point). Demonstrations were fixed and not used as test samples. In one-shot, a random demonstration from the same task was used, while in few-shot, all demonstrations were included in a consistent random order. Each prompt ended with the assistant message formatted as "Level: " to ensure the next token predicted was the proficiency level. The example of a one-shot prompt used in this study is shown in Figure 3. [3]

4.2 Response Characteristics Analysis

To understand what makes the model uncertain, we test whether the characteristics of samples with matching hard and soft labels differ significantly from those with different labels, using Mann-Whitney U tests across zero-, one-, and few-shot settings.

[2] https://huggingface.co/meta-llama/Llama-3.1-8B-Instruct

[3] The code and prompt variables are available at https://github.com/katildakat/LLM_ASA_SOFT_LABELS.

5 Results

5.1 Proficiency Scoring and Model Uncertainty

Table 2 presents proficiency scoring results measured by accuracy (Acc), macro F1, QWK, and macro mean absolute error (MAE). Macro indicates that the metric was computed for responses in each level and then averaged to boost the influence of the underrepresented classes for the final score. The table also includes how often soft labels are closer to the true label than hard labels (denoted as "S wins") shown as fractions (e.g., 10/30 means soft labels were closer in 10 out of 30 cases where soft and hard labels differ). It also includes the average model uncertainty, quantified by the entropy H of the probability distribution over level tokens.

The results show that ICL approaches consistently outperform zero-shot, with performance improving as the number of examples increases. Few-shot learning achieves the best results across all metrics. Notably, model uncertainty increases with the number of demonstrations (the entropy rises from 0.75 in zero-shot to 1.19 in few-shot). This growing uncertainty aligns with an increasing benefit of soft labeling: in zero-shot, hard labels outperform soft labels most of the time (12/49), but soft labeling shows a slight advantage in one-shot (23/40) and a substantial improvement in few-shot (74/117). These trends are reflected in other performance metrics, highlighting the value of soft labeling when paired with few-shot ICL.

	Acc↑	F1↑	QWK↑	MAE↓	S wins	H
z_H	.26	.15	.21	1.63		
z_S	.24	.14	.23	1.68	12/49	0.75
o_H	.24	.18	.39	1.34		
o_S	.26	.18	.43	1.29	23/40	0.86
f_H	.31	.24	.61	1.05		
f_S	**.36**	**.30**	**.67**	**0.93**	74/117	1.19

Table 2: Proficiency scoring results with hard (H) and soft (S) labeling. Metrics include accuracy (Acc), macro F1, QWK (↑ better), and macro MAE (↓ better). "S wins" shows how often soft labels outperform hard labels, and H denotes model uncertainty (entropy). z_H/S, o_H/S, and f_H/S represent zero-, one-, and few-shot learning, respectively.

Figure 4 shows the average probability distributions of proficiency label tokens across zero-, one-, and few-shot settings, illustrating how model uncertainty evolves with increasing contextual information. Each line represents the model's predicted probabilities for a true proficiency level. In zero-shot, the distribution is narrow, with most responses concentrated around level 3, reflecting lower uncertainty and more conservative decisions. As more examples are provided, the distributions spread out, with few-shot showing the widest divergence and highest entropy. This increased uncertainty in few-shot settings enables more nuanced and less deterministic decision-making, which is also why soft labeling differs most significantly from hard labeling in this setting.

5.2 Response Characteristics Analysis

Table 3 compares the characteristics of responses where hard and soft labels match to those where they differ. This analysis aims to identify the properties of a sample that make the model less confident in predicting a single level during evaluation. The arrow direction in the table indicates whether the characteristic value increases (↑) or decreases (↓) for samples where soft labeling diverges from hard labeling.

Entropy is included as a sanity check to ensure that the model exhibits higher uncertainty for samples where soft labels differ from hard labels, and indeed, the results show that entropy is consistently higher (↑) across all ICL settings. This aligns with expectations, as higher uncertainty allows non-dominant classes to shift the probability away from the dominant label. The factors driving this uncertainty vary across settings: in zero-shot, both perplexity (↑) and CEFR score (↓) significantly influence entropy. In one-shot, none of the other tested characteristics show significant differences. In few-shot, cosine distance (↓) emerges as a key factor, indicating that responses closer to the demonstrations tend to have higher uncertainty

6 Discussion

Our results confirm previous findings (Brown, 2020) that ICL outperforms zero-shot, with performance improving as more demonstrations are added. The best setup (few-shot with soft labeling) achieves human-level agreement, reaching a QWK of 0.67 compared to 0.73 for human raters. A macro MAE of just 1 point indicates reliable differentiation between proficiency levels. While

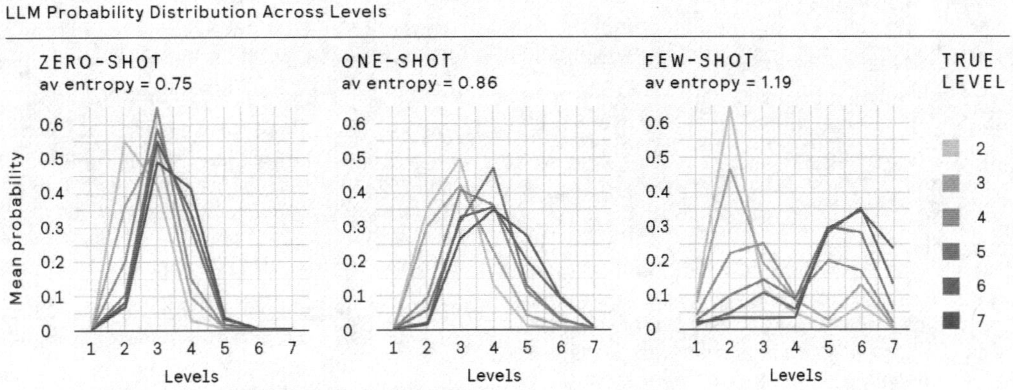

Figure 4: Average probability distributions for zero-, one-, and few-shot settings.

	zero	one	few
entropy	✓↑	✓↑	✓↑
ppl	✓↑	✗	✗
human variance	✗	✗	✗
cosine distance	–	✗	✓↓
CEFR level	✓↓	✗	✗

Table 3: Comparison of response characteristics for samples where hard and soft labels match versus those where they differ. Rows represent characteristics and columns represent ICL settings (zero-, one-, few-shot). Arrows indicate whether the characteristic increases (↑) or decreases (↓) for samples with differing soft and hard labels.

accuracy and macro F1 remain modest, this reflects the data's challenging nature, even for human raters.

In ICL, entropy increases with more demonstrations, yet this added uncertainty enhances performance, particularly with soft labeling. We suspect that higher entropy indicates the model's learning of proficiency level cues. Interestingly, in few-shot settings, entropy is higher when demonstrations are closer to the test sample, even though closer examples do improve predictions (Liu et al., 2021), one would expect this to occur with less uncertainty, not more.

Consistent with (Sánchez et al., 2024), we find a negative correlation between perplexity and CEFR levels (-0.59 Spearman r) and a positive correlation between perplexity and WER (0.75 Spearman r), suggesting that beginner learners tend to produce speech that deviates more from what LLMs and ASR models consider well-formed. However, high perplexity (and thus WER) only affects predictions in zero-shot, where the model becomes uncertain and acts as a severe rater according to its bias. In ICL, perplexity does not influence uncertainty, as the model relies on the relationship between the sample and the demonstrations to base its decisions on.

Surprisingly, human disagreement did not affect the LLM's decisions. This could be due to the study's limitations: the models only had access to ASR transcripts, which serve as proxies for pronunciation and fluency. Delivery features that may contribute to human score variance were not available.

7 Conclusion

This study shows that LLMs can effectively grade Finnish L2 speech in a few-shot setting, achieving QWK scores comparable to human raters, with soft labeling being especially beneficial. More demonstrations in ICL increase entropy, enhancing performance in few-shot prompting. In ICL, perplexity does not influence scoring decisions; rather, the model's uncertainty is shaped by the relationship between the sample and demonstrations, suggesting that closer proximity in the embedding space helps the model identify nuanced cues. We think that soft labeling can be valuable not only for language proficiency scoring but also for other ordinal classification tasks. Future work will focus on fine-tuning the model to include Finland Swedish and incorporating delivery features directly to LLMs to improve grading accuracy.

Acknowledgements

This work was funded by Research Council of Finland's grants 322625, 345790, 355587 and 365233. The computational resources were provided by Aalto ScienceIT.

References

Ragheb Al-Ghezi, Yaroslav Getman, Ekaterina Voskoboinik, Mittul Singh, and Mikko Kurimo. 2023. Automatic rating of spontaneous speech for low-resource languages. In *2022 IEEE Spoken Language Technology Workshop (SLT)*, pages 339–345. IEEE.

Alexei Baevski, Yuhao Zhou, Abdelrahman Mohamed, and Michael Auli. 2020. wav2vec 2.0: A framework for self-supervised learning of speech representations. *Advances in neural information processing systems*, 33:12449–12460.

Stefano Bannò and Marco Matassoni. 2023. Proficiency assessment of l2 spoken english using wav2vec 2.0. In *2022 IEEE Spoken Language Technology Workshop (SLT)*, pages 1088–1095. IEEE.

Jared Bernstein, Jian Cheng, and Masanori Suzuki. 2010. Fluency and structural complexity as predictors of l2 oral proficiency. In *Eleventh annual conference of the international speech communication association*.

Tom B Brown. 2020. Language models are few-shot learners. *arXiv preprint arXiv:2005.14165*.

Lei Chen, Jidong Tao, Shabnam Ghaffarzadegan, and Yao Qian. 2018. End-to-end neural network based automated speech scoring. In *2018 IEEE international conference on acoustics, speech and signal processing (ICASSP)*, pages 6234–6238. IEEE.

Miao Chen and Klaus Zechner. 2011. Computing and evaluating syntactic complexity features for automated scoring of spontaneous non-native speech. In *Proceedings of the 49th annual meeting of the Association for Computational Linguistics: Human Language Technologies*, pages 722–731.

Council of Europe. 2001. *Common European Framework of Reference for Languages: Learning, teaching, assessment*. Cambridge University Press.

Jacob Devlin. 2018. Bert: Pre-training of deep bidirectional transformers for language understanding. *arXiv preprint arXiv:1810.04805*.

Masamune Kobayashi, Masato Mita, and Mamoru Komachi. 2024. Large language models are state-of-the-art evaluator for grammatical error correction. *arXiv preprint arXiv:2403.17540*.

Jiachang Liu, Dinghan Shen, Yizhe Zhang, Bill Dolan, Lawrence Carin, and Weizhu Chen. 2021. What makes good in-context examples for gpt-3? *arXiv preprint arXiv:2101.06804*.

Tin Lun, Ekaterina Voskoboinik, Ragheb Al-Ghezi, Tamás Grósz, and Mikko Kurimo. 2024. https://doi.org/10.21437/Interspeech.2024-760 Oversampling, augmentation and curriculum learning for speaking assessment with limited training data. pages 4019–4023.

Ali Malik, Stephen Mayhew, Chris Piech, and Klinton Bicknell. 2024. From tarzan to tolkien: Controlling the language proficiency level of llms for content generation. *arXiv preprint arXiv:2406.03030*.

Yao Qian, Patrick Lange, Keelan Evanini, Robert Pugh, Rutuja Ubale, Matthew Mulholland, and Xinhao Wang. 2019. Neural approaches to automated speech scoring of monologue and dialogue responses. In *ICASSP 2019-2019 IEEE international conference on acoustics, speech and signal processing (ICASSP)*, pages 8112–8116. IEEE.

Alec Radford, Jeff Wu, Rewon Child, David Luan, Dario Amodei, and Ilya Sutskever. 2019. Language models are unsupervised multitask learners.

Ricardo Muñoz Sánchez, Simon Dobnik, and Elena Volodina. 2024. Harnessing gpt to study second language learner essays: Can we use perplexity to determine linguistic competence? In *Proceedings of the 19th Workshop on Innovative Use of NLP for Building Educational Applications (BEA 2024)*, pages 414–427.

Hugo Touvron, Louis Martin, Kevin Stone, Peter Albert, Amjad Almahairi, Yasmine Babaei, Nikolay Bashlykov, Soumya Batra, Prajjwal Bhargava, Shruti Bhosale, et al. 2023. Llama 2: Open foundation and fine-tuned chat models. *arXiv preprint arXiv:2307.09288*.

Ashish Vaswani, Noam Shazeer, Niki Parmar, Jakob Uszkoreit, Llion Jones, Aidan N Gomez, Łukasz Kaiser, and Illia Polosukhin. 2017. Attention is all you need. *Advances in Neural Information Processing Systems*, 30.

Xinhao Wang, Keelan Evanini, Yao Qian, and Matthew Mulholland. 2021. Automated scoring of spontaneous speech from young learners of english using transformers. In *2021 IEEE spoken language technology workshop (SLT)*, pages 705–712. IEEE.

Shasha Xie, Keelan Evanini, and Klaus Zechner. 2012. Exploring content features for automated speech scoring. In *Proceedings of the 2012 conference of the North American chapter of the Association for Computational Linguistics: Human language technologies*, pages 103–111.

Su-Youn Yoon and Chungmin Lee. 2019. Content modeling for automated oral proficiency scoring system. In *Proceedings of the fourteenth workshop on innovative use of NLP for building educational applications*, pages 394–401.

Klaus Zechner, Derrick Higgins, Xiaoming Xi, and David M. Williamson. 2009. https://api.semanticscholar.org/CorpusID:27619107 Automatic scoring of non-native spontaneous speech in tests of spoken english. *Speech Commun.*, 51:883–895.